YOUR KNOWLEDGE HAS VALUE

- - We will publish your bachelor's and master's thesis, essays and papers

- - Your own eBook and book - sold worldwide in all relevant shops

- - Earn money with each sale

Upload your text at www.GRIN.com and publish for free

Bibliographic information published by the German National Library:

The German National Library lists this publication in the National Bibliography; detailed bibliographic data are available on the Internet at http://dnb.dnb.de .

Imprint:

Copyright © 2019 GRIN Verlag
Print and binding: Books on Demand GmbH, Norderstedt Germany
ISBN: 9783668986374

This book at GRIN:

https://www.grin.com/document/491408

Gabriel Kabanda

Trends in Information Technology Management

GRIN Verlag

TRENDS IN INFORMATION TECHNOLOGY MANAGEMENT

Gabriel Kabanda

Atlantic International University

ABSTRACT

The paper presents an analytical exposition, critical context and integrative conclusion on the trends and best practices in Information Technology Management, and reviews and evaluates the key issues, trends and future direction of Modern Information Technology Management. IT is generally accepted as a key enabler of economic and technological growth. Managers implement new technology to change something: the organization, the nature of work, relationships with other organizations, or some other facet of business. Information Technology (IT) plays a vital role in leveraging productivity and efficiency in private organizations, governments and research. The value of IT in any organization depends on its infrastructure, which consists of computers, network and telecommunication technologies, data and core software applications. Information Technology (IT) is now a force and driver of modern technological development and globalization, and makes the management of information more efficient and effective. Technology management entails all management activities that determine the application of policy, objectives and responsibilities as well as their execution in an organization in terms of planning, allocating resources, organizing and ensuring outcomes that improve processes. The major IT Management issues are: Using technology to design efficient and effective organizations; Developing a plan for information technology in the organization; Using IT as a part of corporate strategy; Taking advantage of interorganizational systems; Deciding on and developing new applications of IT; Reengineering business processes; Adopting special applications; Changing the organization; Managing the IT infrastructure in a time of explosive growth and technological change; Deciding whether and what to outsource; and Deciding how much to invest in IT. Knowledge and skills are a necessary and sufficient condition for technological progress. Developing countries lack enough skilled IT persons who can design, program, install, configure and maintain Information Technology in this constantly changing industry. Accordingly, lack of qualified and globally recognized IT professionals is seriously hampering IT adoption and development. Management Information Systems refer to information management methods tied to the automation or support of human decision making, whereas IT Management refers to the IT related management activities in organizations.

Table of contents

1. ANALYTICAL EXPOSITION 1

2. CRITICAL CONTEXT 6

3. INTEGRATIVE CONCLUSION 11

References... 14

1. ANALYTICAL EXPOSITION

The paper presents an analytical exposition, critical context and integrative conclusion on the trends and best practices in Information Technology Management, and reviews and evaluates the key issues, trends and future direction of *Modern Information Technology Management*. The introduction of computers and communication technologies and their constant improvements have transformed the way organisations behave and conduct business. The importance of information technology cannot be over emphasized. Information technology is at the epicenter of global socio- economic transformation and is a strategic resource and foundation for every economic activity (Kabanda, G., 2014). According to Stallings, W. (2005), any business that ignores this fact will fall hopelessly behind in the global race for the competitive edge. While Stallings, W. (2005)'s assertion is true, developing countries face many challenges in trying to catch up with global trends and thus they will mostly occupy the tail end in this respect. Generally African countries are largely end consumers of technology and lag even further behind in terms of ICT innovations (Kabanda, G., 2014).

Information Technology (IT) is the set of tools for acquisition, processing, storage and dissemination of vocal, pictorial, textual and numerical information by a microelectronics-based combination of computing, telecommunications and video. In general IT represents the convergence of all types of computer equipment, certain electronic (audio and video) equipment, all types of software for use with computers, telecommunications equipment and software, and other automation techniques. The term information and communications technology (ICT) is generally used and usually refers to the integration of information and telecommunication technology sectors involving their convergence with the media technology sector based on common digital technology. ICT includes all types of telecommunication and broadcasting systems and services (wireline, wireless, mobile, satellite), computer hardware, software, networks and services, content producing and managing multimedia systems (Sallai, G., 2012, p.6). ICT, therefore, means any communication device, application, or service related to radio, television, cellular technology, computing, networking, and satellite systems, including services such as videoconferencing and distance learning. ICT has a tremendous impact on reducing costs and increasing the quality of management of business processes. Berisha-Shaqiri, A. (2015, p.166) argued that ICT has gained great importance when it comes to the success and efficiency of business helping business processes in the following areas:

❖ Information Technology positively affects the reduction of management costs, because its application improves the quality of management;

❖ In addition to revenue growth, ICT facilitates the communication between managers, by saving time and quality of communication within the enterprise;

❖ Through internal network and enterprise information the distribution between workers and managers at the right time and at the same time also affects the growth of their knowledge;

❖ ICT affects the reduction of workers in occupations where knowledge is not required;

❖ ICT increases the demand for knowledge workers;

❖ ICT and the use of computer networks affects revenue growth.

Modern information systems are largely driven by the development of the internet. The internet revolutionized how the world communicates, stores and accesses information. 'Faster computers and cheaper storage are useful in their own right. But the reason that all of these technologies have had such a massive impact on almost all aspects of life is that these devices are linked so that information can be distributed and accessed effortlessly from anywhere.' (World Bank Report, 2016, p.42). This development has brought with it several issues, positive and negative. The speed of development of technology has increased exponentially over the last three decades since the invention of the World Wide Web (WWW) in 1989. The ease of sharing and accessing information across the globe has enabled technology developers to reduce their development time. The internet brought with it inclusivity, helping to integrate African countries with the rest of the world digitally. 'Inclusion for the individual usually means expansion of a market by those on the other side of the transaction, such as a firm or a government that now serves more citizens', (World Bank Report, 2016, p.43).

The practice of technology management requires a better theoretical structure to avoid being blindsided by new technology (Dolinsek, S., and Strukelj, P., 2012, p.30). In the world of investments, monies flow in and out of technology-based companies more on the basis of fashion than on the basis of rational technology analysis. According to Dolinsek, S., and Strukelj, P. (2012, p.31) technology is a large and growing part of every manager's daily experience, where managers develop technology, use technology, buy technology and sell technology. On the contrary, the common observation is that key management decision makers have inadequate background and ability to make judgments and forecasts in the area of technology; and without that ability, their options in utilizing technology in corporate strategy are severely limited. Technology is addressed in strategic plans only implicitly, except in the case of special endeavors which are outside the main lines of production. Strategic management of technology and innovation is a young field and the domains of different in developing nations. Khalil (2012) cited in Dolinsek, S., and Strukelj, P. (2012, p.32) proposed a conception that any technology consists of four interdependent, codetermining, and equally important components:

➢ *Hardware*: The physical structure and logical layout of the equipment or machinery that is to be used to carry out the required tasks.
➢ *Software:* The knowledge of how to use the hardware in order to carry out the required tasks.
➢ *Brainware:* The reasons for using the technology in a particular way.
➢ *Know-how:* which covers the skills and technological achievements.

Computers have enhanced the speed and ease of communication between individuals and companies. Ideas spread quickly and easily, cutting across geographical boundaries at low cost. Companies save time and money in implementing their strategies as more and more transactions like sales and purchases are implemented over the phone or on the internet and managers are quickly aided in their decision making processes. Distributed information processing is used in most companies for both intra-company and inter-company exchange. Technology has also improved production in almost every industry in the world. It is used in the health sector in a way that has saved many lives and improved the quality of life and longevity (Stallings, W., 2005). Machines now carry out a lot of the work in the industrial and agricultural sectors and have led to increased outputs. Technology has provided better working environments, reduced human effort and improved efficiencies. With more technological advances taking place, organisations are able to store more information in smaller spaces and retrieve information at higher speeds. On the educational front, technology has improved access to knowledge and enhanced research efforts. The four types of information namely voice, data, image and video technology are dominating factors in shaping the competitiveness of enterprises (Gudanowska, A.E.,2017).

Knowledge and skills are a necessary and sufficient condition for technological progress. Without knowledge and skills, machines, devices and processes of production would be just some unknown, unuseful, arbitrary and coincidental processes and pieces of material. Knowledge and skills are fundamental to consistently use machines, devices and processes of production rationally and effectively. According to Dolinsek, S., and Strukelj, P. (2012, p.35), technology refers to:
➢ machines and devices that are used in manufacturing (processing), storing and delivering of material products, energy and information,
➢ processes (with the use of machinery and devices) of manufacturing (processing), storing and delivering material products, energy and information,
➢ devices and their processes that are included as components in final products,
➢ advanced functional materials,
➢ most generally, devices that people and organizations use in their activities.

Dolinsek, S., and Strukelj, P. (2012, p.36) introduced a principal relationship between technology and wealth, which states that by inventing, developing technologies, by using them and by advancing, improving them, we can:
➢ produce existing goods more efficiently,
➢ produce more goods,
➢ produce better goods,
➢ produce new goods,
➢ save labor (though development, maintenance and advancement of technology requires labor) and increase leisure/spare time,
➢ make labor easier,
➢ improve goods,
➢ make activities easier,
➢ enable new activities.

How and to what extent a technology contributes to wealth in a society depends on the principles of the socio-economic order in that society, in which technology is developed, used and advanced. Technological capability is one of the central elements in the practice of technology management.

Theory in management of technology should therefore pay sufficient attention to this phenomenon and provide some satisfying results. Technological capability refers to our capability (capacity) to use technologies (as well as knowledge and skills necessary for their proper use) in a way that contributes to effective and successful achievement of our purposes. Technological capability is not the same as technology or as knowledge and skills of how to use a technology in order to produce a desired product. Technological capability is our competence/capacity to purposefully use technology and the necessary knowledge and skills (Dolinsek, S., and Strukelj, P., 2012, p.41). Technological capability refers both to individuals and organizations/institutions, i.e., an individual as well as an organization/institution can have a technological capability.

According to Gallon *et al* (1995) cited in Dolinsek, S., and Strukelj, P. (2012, p.41), technological capabilities are then divided into:

➢ applied science capabilities (fundamental know-how derived from basic research),

➢ design and development capabilities (disciplines employed in converting a product idea into an operational reality),

➢ manufacturing capabilities (capabilities employed in, or directly supporting, established manufacturing or operations).

Management of technology links engineering, science and management disciplines to plan, develop, and implement technological capabilities to shape and accomplish the strategic and operational objectives of an organization. Managing technology implies managing the systems that enable the creation, acquisition and exploitation of technology. Management of technology is organizing, coordinating and leading the use/handling of technology (and technological knowledge and skills) in an organization. According to Dolinsek, S., and Strukelj, P. (2012, p.43), management of technology involves the following basic activities:

➢ planning of the use of technology,

➢ identification, selection and acquisition of technology,

➢ preparation and introduction of the use of technology,

➢ implementation, installation and control of the use of technology,

➢ motivating and maintaining the use of technology.

➢ technology auditing,

➢ scanning the technological environment and analyzing technology trends,

➢ technology forecasting and technology foresight,

➢ formulation of technology strategy,

➢ technology transfer,

➢ technology development.

However, developing countries usually lack the required resources for technological improvement. Employees need to be trained and retrained with every new breakthrough. According to Schiller, B.R. (2003), technological advances shrink the labour force while increasing output. The Behavioural Theory suggests that information systems could change the hierarchy of decision making thus reducing the need of middle management and clerical support to distribute information (Kabanda, G., 2019).

The modern practice of management of technology should take the following trends into account:

➤ production economies of scope are equally important with economies of scale, and production automation should be appropriately balanced between hard and soft automation (depending upon product volumes and product lifetimes),

➤ multi-core-technology product lines will have shorter product life times and should be planned as generations of products (paced by the most rapidly changing critical technology), and the organization must be flexibly organized for rapid and correct response,

➤ world markets and technology are now global, and enterprises should be globally based to 'think globally and act locally'.

Information Technology Management is concerned with exploring and understanding Information Technology as a corporate resource that determines both the strategic and operational capabilities of the firm in designing and developing products and services for maximum customer satisfaction, corporate productivity, profitability and competitiveness (Catalin, P., and Alina, P., 2010, p.1). Management Information Systems refer to information management methods tied to the automation or support of human decision making, whereas IT Management refers to the IT related management activities in organizations.

Information Technology Management is heavily dependent upon the alignment of technology and business strategies, and includes considering the value creation that is created through technology. Technology plays an important role in improving the overall value chain of an organization, where the value creation for an organization is a network of relationships between internal and external environments. The IT Manager and the Project Manager have a lot in Common as both work to achieve organizational goals by directing the activities of people. According to Catalin, P., and Alina, P. (2010, p.2), the IT Manager is responsible for an ongoing program of IT services, while the Project Manager's accountability and authority last only for the life of the project. Hence, it is the time-limited nature of projects that makes the role of Project Manager so important. What every IT Manager needs to know about Project Management is that there are best practices which when socialized into an organization can greatly enhance the success of projects. Therefore, adopting Project Management will make the work of effectively managing change in the IT environment easier and more consistent.

2. CRITICAL CONTEXT

Information Technology (IT) is now a force and driver of modern technological development and globalization, and makes the management of information more efficient and effective (Ejiaku, S.A., 2014, p.61). IT is generally accepted as a key enabler of economic and technological growth. Information Technology has unlimited potential to improve business operations, education, technology and economic growth. However, this technology could help contribute to poverty alleviation in developing economies if used to meet local and national needs. Information Technology (IT) plays a vital role in leveraging productivity and efficiency in private organizations, governments and research.The value of IT in any organization depends on its infrastructure, which consists of computers, network and telecommunication technologies, data and core software applications. Developing countries lack enough skilled IT persons who can design, program, install, configure and maintain Information Technology in this constantly changing industry (Ejiaku, S.A., 2014, p.62). Accordingly, lack of qualified and globally recognized IT professionals is seriously hampering IT adoption and development. Ejiaku, S.A. (2014, p.63) observed that ineffective government policies, poor infrastructure and inadequate training and qualification are contributory factors in creating challenges in IT transfer and adoption in Africa.IT Management must take into cognisance all these challenges and issues, especially in developing economies. Managers implement new technology to change something: the organization, the nature of work, relationships with other organizations, or some other facet of business (Lucas, H.C., 2009, p.x).

Technology management entails all management activities that determine the application of policy, objectives and responsibilities as well as their execution in an organization in terms of planning, allocating resources, organizing and ensuring outcomes that improve processes (Laudon, K.C., and Traver, C.G., 2008). Gudanowska, A.E. (2017), concurs adding that technology management should take into account the resources available, currently used technology, the future of the market and the social and economic environments. According to Kabanda, G., (2019), there are relevant that theories can be used to evaluate the impact of technology in an organization or country. The first one is the Microeconomic Model which looks at technology as a factor of production like labour and capital. The Cobb-Douglas production function is used to explain the relationship between the inputs of labour and capital to produce the output which can be significantly increased if technology is added as another form of input (Walsh, C., 2003).

A CEO understands the role and importance of information technology in managing a twenty-first century organization. Lucas, S.A. (2009, p.7) posits that IT
➤ Provides new ways to design organizations and new organizational structures.
➤ Creates new relationships between customers and suppliers who electronically link themselves together.
➤ Presents the opportunity for electronic commerce, which reduces purchasing cycle times, increases the exposure of suppliers to customers, and creates greater convenience for buyers.
➤ Enables tremendous efficiencies in production and service industries through electronic data interchange to facilitate just-in-time production.
➤ Changes the basis of competition and industry structure, for example, in the airline and securities industries.
➤ Provides mechanisms through groupware for coordinating work and creating a knowledge base of organizational intelligence.

➢ Makes it possible for the organization to capture the knowledge of its employees and provide access to it throughout the organization.
➢ Contributes to the productivity and flexibility of knowledge workers.
➢ Provides the manager with electronic alternatives to face-to-face communications and supervision.
➢ Provides developing countries with opportunities to compete with the industrialized nations.

Managers delegate tasks and decision making to lower levels of management, and information systems make data available at the level of management where it is needed to make decisions (Lucas, S.A., 2009, p.14). Technology-enabled firms feature highly automated production and electronic information handling to minimize the use of paper and rely extensively on images and optical data storage. According to Lucas, S.A. (2009, p.15), managers are challenged with decisions about:
❖ The use of technology to design and structure the organization.
❖ The creation of alliances and partnerships that include electronic linkages.
❖ The selection of systems to support different kinds of workers.
❖ The adoption of groupware or group-decision support systems for workers who share a common task.
❖ Determining a World Wide Web strategy.
❖ Routine transactions processing systems.
❖ Personal support systems.
❖ Reporting and control.
❖ Automated production processes.
❖ Embedded products.

Information Technology (IT), demands design, installation, configuration, training and maintenance of infrastructure (Ejiaku, S.A., 2014). Continuous IT adoption and development, in varying degrees is necessary in both developing and developed countries because IT is a major driver of modern technological development and globalization. Watson and Meyers (2001) identify three major factors that impact on the development of a successful IT industry in a developed country. These are the extent of IT promotion by governments, the level of research and development, and the existence of an education system that produces IT literate graduates. In developing countries, lack of resources to develop IT in their respective countries and a heavy dependence on foreign aid are important factors that impact on development. Poor basic IT infrastructure and networks in developing countries also hamper their ability to facilitate adequate IT transfer, implementation and development.

IT brings tremendous changes with resect to the following areas (Lucas, S.A., 2009, p.17):
❖ Within organizations
  Create new procedures, workflows, workgroups, the knowledge base, prod?ucts and services, and communications.
❖ Organizational structure
  Facilitate new reporting relationships, increased spans of control, local deci?sion rights, supervision, the formation of divisions, geographic scope, and
  "virtual" organizations.
❖ Interorganizational relations
  Create new customer-supplier relations, partnerships, and alliances.

❖ The economy
   Alter the nature of markets through electronic commerce, disintermediation, new forms of marketing and advertising, partnerships and alliances, the cost of transactions, and modes of governance in customer-supplier relationships.
❖ Education
   Enhance "on campus" education through videoconferencing, e-mail, electronic meet?ings, groupware, and electronic guest lectures.
   Facilitate distance learning through e-mail, groupware, and videoconferencing.
   Provide access to vast amounts of reference material; facilitate collaborative projects independent of time zones and distance.
❖ National development
   Provide small companies with international presence and facilitate commerce.
   Make large amounts of information available, perhaps to the consternation of cer?tain governments.
   Present opportunities to improve education.

Information technology today provides computational and communications capabilities that were inconceivable a decade ago. A manager has to know enough about technology to take advantage of the power IT offers. The major IT Management issues, according to Lucas, S.A. (2009, p.20), are :
➢ Using technology to design efficient and effective organizations
➢ Developing a plan for information technology in the organization
➢ Using IT as a part of corporate strategy
➢ Taking advantage of interorganizational systems
➢ Deciding on and developing new applications of IT
➢ Reengineering business processes
➢ Adopting special applications
➢ Changing the organization
➢ Managing the IT infrastructure in a time of explosive growth and technological change
➢ Deciding whether and what to outsource
➢ Deciding how much to invest in IT

Lucas, S.A. (2009, p.135) presented the following strategies to manage Global IT:
➢ Concentrate on interorganizational linkages
➢ Establish global systems development skills
➢ Build an infrastructure
➢ Take advantage of liberalized telecommunications
➢ Strive for uniform data
➢ Develop guidelines for shared versus local systems

Due to rapid technological changes, we now witness a phenomenal growth of global companies. A global company should have the following features:
➢ Treats the world as a single market.
➢ More products sold outside the home country than within the home country.
➢ Worldwide sourcing of customers, employees, suppliers and technology--sourcing with a total dis?regard for national boundaries

Technology management is an emerging field that combines multiple disciplines and can be defined in terms of identification, selection, acquisition, and exploitation as an ongoing process. Organizational performance is influenced by how strategies are implemented and the role technology plays in creating sustainable business models. Organizations learning to manage technology with internal and external sources and competing in complex and technological environments reach a critical point in obtaining knowledge. Management of technology education covers strategic management, project management, R&D management, new product development, innovation management, entrepreneurship, and information management. These types of management are interconnected and interdependent on each other. Processing and storage capacities are rising exponentially, and knowledge is becoming accessible to more people than ever before in human history. The future holds an even higher potential for human development as the full effects of new technologies such as the Internet of Things, artificial
intelligence, 3-D Printing, energy storage, and quantum computing unfold.

Artificial intelligence (AI) is one of the biggest areas of focus for future technology development. To make execution of tasks faster, simpler and cheaper, organisations are continuously exploring ways of enabling machines to do more and more of what humans currently do. This has the impact of reducing operational costs in the long run, while at the same time eliminating the need for some jobs held by humans. 'Machines are becoming smarter in that they can learn how to solve problems. One such system is a neural network, which is used to alert you that your credit card may have been used unlawfully,' (Cummings, M., 2012). Neural networks develop trends or patterns of user behaviour over time. When activity that is outside the normal pattern is detected, the neural network raises an alarm. These systems are growing in use in many different fields and will provide greater support to human beings in rapid decision making. As much as these developments positively impact MIS, they also affect people's cultures, raise legal questions in some areas and possibly national security concerns.

Terabytes of data are being created everyday globally, what is being referred as Big Data, and its storage and management is becoming increasingly complex with time. Its analysis and subsequent use has legal implications when it involves third parties. Lawyers will increasingly be burdened with the responsibility of determining what is legal and what is not from a privacy point of view. Banks across the world are setting up Compliance departments to manage among other issues, the collection, storage and usage of stakeholder information. It is the job of the Compliance department to ensure that MIS is in place to filter such clients from receiving international banking services that may result in heavy fines being imposed on the institution for violation.

Rainer, R.K. (2012) states that the following are the emerging technologies of the future: Artificial Intelligence (AI), Internet of Things (IoT), Blockchain, Financial Technology (FinTech) and Quantum Computing. The Internet of Things (IoT) is growing phenomenally. Almost any object that has some form of electrical current flowing through it will in future have sensors installed. These sensors will be linked to some system via the internet for various purposes, 'the rapid increase of placing sensors on all objects (animate and inanimate) is leading to a sense-and-respond environment', (Rainer, R.K., 2012).

Blockchain, or Distributed-ledger technology is developing into many areas of business, the most common currently is Cryptocurrency. This is disrupting the traditional regulated financial services system. This is an unregulated financial currency with no geographical jurisdiction as well. Most people are still sceptical about cryptocurrencies, governments are concerned about how it cannot be regulated, thereby making it difficult to deal with money-laundering, terrorism financing and sanctions busting transactions. This increases the need for organisations to closely monitor how these developments will impact them.

For decades, digital computing has been about bits which are either a '0' or a '1'. Quantum Computing uses quantum bits (qubits), which can exist in any superposition of these values. It is still in its infancy, but the potential will provide a significant increase in computing speeds and vary computing parameters further without being limited to two states of '1' and '0'. Quantum computing is helping to improve other advanced technologies, such a Genetic Algorithms. These two have been combined to produce Quantum Genetic Algorithms (QGA), 'The efficiency of QGA is significantly better than the conventional genetic algorithm. The QGA is with a small value of the population, a fast speed of convergence, a great capability of global optimization, and a good robustness', (Wang, H., *et al*, 2013, p.1). as digital was a revolutionary development from analogue, quantum computing, once completely figured out, will be just as revolutionary from digital.

Sakovich, N. (2018), and Weldon, D. (2018), identify the following technological developments for 2019 and beyond:

1) **Cloud Computing** - According to Sakovich, N. (2018), more and more enterprises will have computing infrastructure in the cloud. The trend will actually lean towards the use of multi-clouds. With increased IT spending, there will be more breakthroughs in mobile internet which will affect cloud computing and stimulate other innovations.

2) **Artificial Intelligence (AI)** - AI will expand its presence in many sectors, making its way into more homes and offices and will be integrated in transport systems, healthcare, finance and education. AI will reshape the labour market causing some professions to disappear and new relevant ones to appear (Sakovich, N., 2018).

3) **5th Generation Wireless (5G)** - New generation networks and 5G smartphones are expected to bring broadband download speeds over mobile networks and provide 10x faster internet services than 4G. According to Sakovich, N. (2018), the use of new generation networks will be much wider with 5G providing impetus for further developments.

4) **Internet of Things** - This the network of physical devices, vehicles, home appliances and many other items embedded with electronics, software sensors actuators and connectivity which enable these objects to connect and exchange data.

5) **Automation** - There will be widespread use of technology by which procedures are performed without human assistance. These include self-driven cars and robotic surgery.

6) **Drones** – These unmanned air vehicles or autonomous aircrafts are already being used for military surveillance and accident monitoring in developed countries.

7) **Augmented reality(AR) / Virtual reality (VR)** – AR is a direct or indirect live view of a physical, real world environment. VR is a computer-generated scenario that simulates a realistic experience.

8) **3D Printing** – This is a process where materials are joined or solidified under computer to create three- dimensional objects.

9) **Biometrics** – Future trends will include the wide spread of biometrics or realistic authentication as a form of identification and access control.

10) **Blockchain** – This an information storage system for continuously growing number of records called blocks , which are linked and secured using cryptography.

11) **Quantum Computers** – This is computing using quantum mechanical phenomena such as superposition and entanglement to achieve unprecedented levels of speed.

3. INTEGRATIVE CONCLUSION

The paper presented an analytical exposition, critical context and integrative conclusion on the trends and best practices in Information Technology Management, and reviewed and evaluated the key issues, trends and future direction of *Modern Information Technology Management*. Ejiaku, S.A., (2014) calls for involvement of government by introducing favourable policies, making more training efforts and leading by example in the diffusion and adoption of information technology developments. The private sector can also fully engage in the technological development efforts to enable their countries to experience the benefits that the developed countries are enjoying. The Agency Theory is the third theory that analyses the impact of technology suggesting that one company can introduce new ways of handling transactions and be the nexus or connection point with other smaller players in the market. This will expand the range of services thus perpetuating technology (Kabanda, G., 2019). An example of this in Zimbabwe is Econet which engaged many small players by developing several Ecocash outlets around Zimbabwe to make themselves the leading player in their arena. This same product, Ecocash led to ventures into other new products, within the organization, like Ecosure, Ecosure, Ecocash-Savings club and Ecocash Diaspora. Ecocash enables many transactions including the instant payment of utilities, groceries and other commodities and transfers of cash.

Information Technology (IT) is the set of tools for acquisition, processing, storage and dissemination of vocal, pictorial, textual and numerical information by a microelectronics-based combination of computing, telecommunications and video. The major IT Management issues, according to Lucas, S.A. (2009, p.20), are :

- Using technology to design efficient and effective organizations
- Developing a plan for information technology in the organization
- Using IT as a part of corporate strategy
- Taking advantage of interorganizational systems
- Deciding on and developing new applications of IT
- Reengineering business processes
- Adopting special applications

- Changing the organization
- Managing the IT infrastructure in a time of explosive growth and technological change
- Deciding whether and what to outsource
- Deciding how much to invest in IT

Lucas, S.A. (2009, p.135) presented the following strategies to manage Global IT:

- Concentrate on interorganizational linkages
- Establish global systems development skills
- Build an infrastructure
- Take advantage of liberalized telecommunications
- Strive for uniform data
- Develop guidelines for shared versus local systems

Information Technology Management is concerned with exploring and understanding Information Technology as a corporate resource that determines both the strategic and operational capabilities of the firm in designing and developing products and services for maximum customer satisfaction, corporate productivity, profitability and competitiveness (Catalin, P., and Alina, P., 2010, p.1). Management Information Systems refer to information management methods tied to the automation or support of human decision making, whereas IT Management refers to the IT related management activities in organizations.

ICT has gained great importance when it comes to the success and efficiency of business helping business processes in the following areas:

- Information Technology positively affects the reduction of management costs, because its application improves the quality of management;
- In addition to revenue growth, ICT facilitates the communication between managers, by saving time and quality of communication within the enterprise;
- Through internal network and enterprise information the distribution between workers and managers at the right time and at the same time also affects the growth of their knowledge;
- ICT affects the reduction of workers in occupations where knowledge is not required;
- ICT increases the demand for knowledge workers;
- ICT and the use of computer networks affects revenue growth.

The modern practice of management of technology should take the following trends into account: production economies of scope are equally important with economies of scale, and production automation should be appropriately balanced between hard and soft automation (depending upon product volumes and product lifetimes), multi-core-technology product lines will have shorter product life times and should be planned as generations of products (paced by the most rapidly changing critical technology), and the organization must be flexibly organized for rapid and correct response, world markets and technology are now global, and enterprises should be globally based to 'think globally and act locally'.

Information Technology (IT) is now a force and driver of modern technological development and globalization, and makes the management of information more efficient and effective. IT is generally accepted as a key enabler of economic and technological growth.

Managers implement new technology to change something: the organization, the nature of work, relationships with other organizations, or some other facet of business. Technology management entails all management activities that determine the application of policy, objectives and responsibilities as well as their execution in an organization in terms of planning, allocating resources, organizing and ensuring outcomes that improve processes (Laudon, K.C., and Traver, C.G., 2008). Information Technology (IT) plays a vital role in leveraging productivity and efficiency in private organizations, governments and research.The value of IT in any organization depends on its infrastructure, which consists of computers, network and telecommunication technologies, data and core software applications. Management of technology education covers strategic management, project management, R&D management, new product development, innovation management, entrepreneurship, and information management.

Knowledge and skills are a necessary and sufficient condition for technological progress.Developing countries lack enough skilled IT persons who can design, program, install, configure and maintain Information Technology in this constantly changing industry (Ejiaku, S.A., 2014, p.62). Accordingly, lack of qualified and globally recognized IT professionals is seriously hampering IT adoption and development. Managers delegate tasks and decision making to lower levels of management, and information systems make data available at the level of management where it is needed to make decisions (Lucas, S.A., 2009, p.14). Technology-enabled firms feature highly automated production and electronic information handling to minimize the use of paper and rely extensively on images and optical data storage.

References

BERISHA-SHAQIRI, A., (2015). Information Technology and Management, Academic Journal of Business, Administration, Law and Social Sciences; Voume 1, No 1, March 2015, ISSN 2410-3918, Acces online at www.iipccl.org, IIPCCL Publishing, Tirana-Albania.

CATALIN, P., and Alina, P., (2010). Information Technology Management, Journal of Knowlwdge Management, Economics and Information Technology, http://www.scientificpapers.org.

CUMMINGS, M., (2012). (2012). Management Information Systems for the Information Age. https://www.smartsheet.com/management-information-systems accessed: 14 May 2019.5.15

DOLINSEK, S., and Strukelj, P., (2012). Technology, Wealth and Modern Management of Technology, Volume 10, Number 1, Spring 2012, Managing Global Transitions, University of Primorska, Slovenia.

EJIAKU, S.A., (2014). "Technology Adoption: Issues and Challenges in Information Technology Adoption in Emerging Economies", Journal of International Technology and Information Management, Vol. 23, Issue. 2, Article 5, Available at: http://scholarworks.lib.csusb.edu/jitim/vol23/iss2/5.

GUDANOWSKA, A.E., (2017). Modern Research Trends within Technology Management in the Light of Selected Publications. *Science Direct*. [Online]. Available from www.sciencedirect.com. [Accessed 5/5/19].

KABANDA, G., (2014). Technology Affordances and Diffusion for Mobile Connectivity and Applications in Zimbabwe, *International Journal of Emerging Technology and Advanced Engineering*. *Vol 4; Issue 6, June 2014*, pages 13-23, ISSN 2250–2459 (Online). http://www.ijetae.com/files/Volume4Issue6/IJETAE_0614_116.pdf. [Online]. Available from: www.ijetae.com. [Accessed 10/5/19].

KABANDA, G., (2019). Lecture Notes on '*E-Commerce*', Management Information Systems, Module 12, NUST / ALMA, Mt Pleasant, Harare. 26 April 2019.

LAUDON, K.C., and, Traver, C.G., (2008). (2008). *e-Commerce. Business. Technology. Society*. New Jersey: Pearson: Prentice Hall, Upper Saddle River.

LUCAS, H.C., (2009). Information Technology for Management: A Global Text, Creative Commons Attribution 3.0 License, Switzerland, 2009.

RAINER, R.K., (2012). Management Information Systems, Moving Business Forward. https://www.smartsheet.com/management-information-systems

SAKOVICH, N., (2018). Top Five Information Technology Trends to Watch in 2019. *Sam Solutions*. [Online]. Available from: https://www.sam-solutions.com/blog/top-five-information-technology-trends-to-watch-in-2019/ [Accessed 6/5/19].

SALLAI, G., (2012), Defining InfoCommunications and Related Terms, Acta Polytechnica Hungarian, Volume 9, number 6, 2012.

SCHILER, B. R. (2003). *The Micro-economy Today*. 9th ed. Boston: McGraw – Hill.

STALLINGS, W. (2005). *Business Data Communications*. 5th ed. New Jersey: Pearson - Prentice Hall, Upper Saddle River.

WANG, H., Fu, C., Liu, J., and Zhi, J. (2013). The Improvement of Quantum Genetic Algorithm and Its Application on Function Optimization. Mathematical Problems in Engineering
Volume 2013, Article ID 73074.

WALSH, C. (2003). (2003). *Monetary Theory and Policy*. 2nd ed. Cambridge: MIT Press.

WELDON, D., (2018). *10 Top Technology Trends to Watch in 2019- Information Management*. [Online]. Available from: www.information-management.com/list/10-top-technology-trends/ [Accessed 5/5/19]

WORLD BANK, (2016). World Development Report. Enabling Digital Development. http://documents.worldbank.org/curated/en/896971468194972881/310436360_201602 63021502/additional/102725-PUB-Replacement-PUBLIC.pdf accessed: 13 May 2019

WORLD ECONOMIC FORUM, (2019). https://www.weforum.org/focus/fourth-industrial-revolution accessed: 13 May 2019

YOUR KNOWLEDGE HAS VALUE

- We will publish your bachelor's and
  master's thesis, essays and papers

- Your own eBook and book -
  sold worldwide in all relevant shops

- Earn money with each sale

Upload your text at www.GRIN.com
and publish for free

www.ingramcontent.com/pod-product-compliance
Lightning Source LLC
La Vergne TN
LVHW042128070326
832902LV00037B/1660